# Are You Lost?

## Discover and Realise Your Life Answers

First Edition: 2008


ISBN: 978-1-4092-0031-4

Note: The author (Find My Life Answers Pty Ltd) is not responsible for any liability, loss or risk, personal or otherwise, which is incurred as a result, directly or indirectly, of the use and application of any of the materials discussed in this publication.


For more details about this publication and the company, please visit www.findmylifeanswers.com

# Contents

# Preface

Many of us struggle to find the answers to our life questions. Maybe you are seeking your lifetime goal, career, purpose and/or relationship? When will they arrive? Will you ever achieve them?

It is important that these questions are addressed as finding the answers can significantly change the way you live.

How do you find your life answers? Is there a path that you can take? How do you ensure that these life answers are realised?

This book will explore some of the many pathways that may lead you to discovering and realising your life answers.

# Diagnosis

# Diagnosis

## Are you lost?

Has something been bothering you lately? Unsure about the direction in which your life is heading? Still looking for your lifetime goal, career, purpose and/or relationship? Perhaps it is a larger problem that has been left unresolved for many years.

You have lost patience. You are losing sleep. You can't get the problem out of your head. You are depressed. You have given up!

What should you do?

# Discover Your

# Life Answers

# Discover Your Life Answers

There is no one way or a right way to find the answers to your life questions. Perhaps a starting point is to explore some of the many pathways you can take in finding these answers. There are a number of techniques available and they will be briefly discussed in this section. Once you have found your preferred techniques, it is recommended that you conduct further research to better understand and utilise these methods.

## ❋ Ask Yourself

Don't be surprised, but you may already have the answers to your life questions. All you need to do is to sit down in a quiet corner, relax and reflect on the different ideas floating in your mind. For example, you may want to find out who you really are, what your inner passions are, what makes you happy and/or what you want your life to be.

After spending some time reflecting on these thoughts, you can start to assemble the insights or clues to your life answers.

One great tip to ensure that you capture all of the ideas in your mind is to write them down on a piece of paper. Once they have been written down, you may see part or all of the answers starting to emerge. If they are unclear, look for patterns or themes forming and then draw your conclusions based on what you are seeing.

## ✱ Talk to Someone You Trust

At times, talking to a trusted individual can lead to finding your life answers. For example, you may want to share your thoughts, feelings and concerns. You should find someone who is a good listener or a good sounding board. As you trust the person, you are more inclined to talk openly without the fear of your privacy being exposed.

It is interesting to note that many successful people actively engage a life coach or mentor to seek advice and/or discuss their life matters. Furthermore, having a life coach or mentor can assist in giving encouragement, support and guidance.

## ✱ Learn from Others

Many biographies have been written on people from different walks of life. These books often reveal their periods of 'highs' and 'lows'. It may be interesting to learn the strategies these people employed to achieve success in their lives and how they managed to survive during difficult times.

By reading these stories and reflecting on your life experiences, you may want to adopt some of their strategies and techniques to address your life questions.

# * Meditate

Meditation can help to take your mind away from the present day reality to a chosen or controlled state of mind. To meditate, find a comfortable place and play some relaxing background music. Close your eyes and clear any thoughts that are present in your mind. Once your mind is cleared, introduce a thought around your life question. It is this state of mind that sometimes the clues to your life answers may start to form.

# * Follow a Religion

Following a religion can give you a life mission or purpose. Some religions believe that life revolves around the beliefs and teachings of a god. Other religions may be less god-centric and instead focus on spiritual teachings, self enlightenment, wisdom and compassion.

If you have a religion, try to find your life answers through exploring its beliefs and teachings. You may also want to consult your peers, attend different religious gatherings and conduct research to further understand the religion.

If you do not have a religion but are interested in following this path, do some research to understand the different types available and choose the one which you feel is closely aligned to your belief system.

## ✱ Talk to Your Spirit Guides

Some people believe in the presence of spirit guides. Spirit guides can be people you know that have passed away or those who happen to be around you for whatever reasons.

If you do believe in spirit guides, then talk to them – ask for their guidance and advice. Often they will communicate with you via signs or symbols you see in your dreams or in your present day life.

## ✳ Use Automatic Writing

Automatic writing is a technique which involves letting your mind take control of what you are about to write or draw. To use this technique, firstly you will need to sit down in a quiet corner, consult your spirit guides and ask for their guidance. Then holding a pen, close your eyes and let your mind take control of what your hand is about to write or draw on a piece of paper. Sometimes, you may need to give yourself a few minutes before you experience any hand movements.

The images or writings that you have scribbled down (which may take the form of letters, words, signs, symbols or pictures) may in fact be the clues to your life answers.

## ✳ Contact a Psychic

Some people believe that psychics have the power to fore-tell and predict possible future events. Others are more skeptical.

Sometimes it really does depend on who you are consulting as some can be dubious.

Psychics can use a number of methods to assist you in finding your life answers. These may include the use of intuition, contacting spirits, tarot cards, tea leaves readings, etc.

## ✳ Explore Metaphysical Sciences

Some people believe that metaphysical sciences such as astrology, numerology and palmistry can provide insights into our life. For example, numerology is the study of numbers and how they influence the way you live. Through numerology, you can discover your strengths and weaknesses, life purpose and even future possible events.

As discussed briefly in this section, there are a number of techniques that you can use to find your life answers. Most importantly, choose the techniques that you are most comfortable with as they will deliver the best results for you. Remember, once you have found your preferred techniques, it is recommended that you conduct further research to better understand and utilise these methods.

# Realise Your Life Answers

# Realise Your Life Answers

Assuming that you have now found your life answers using the techniques discussed in the previous section, it is time to make them happen!

So where should you start?

## ✳ Believe in Yourself

As long as you are realistic with your expectations, there is nothing impossible to achieve in life. If you want something, you can have it provided you work towards it. You should never give up if things do not turn out to be what you have expected. If you fail, always learn from the experience as it will only make you stronger and more resilient the next time you try it.

So believe in yourself in achieving your newly discovered life answers.

Sometimes, it can be difficult to pull yourself out of your comfort zone. Perhaps you lack the self confidence or self esteem. You fear the unknown. To overcome this negativity, there are a number of things you can remind yourself:

- ☑ Always look at the positive side of life.
- ☑ You have nothing to lose - if you never try, you will never know.
- ☑ Expect the unexpected e.g. worst case scenario.
- ☑ Do not let yourself 'rot'. Life is too short to sit around and do nothing.
- ☑ Surround yourself with positive people who can give you the encouragement and support.
- ☑ Have confidence in yourself!

## ✱ Make Them Happen

To realise each of your life answers, you may need to follow a series of steps. Remember, no action – no result!

For example, let's say you want to find your life long relationship. You will need to:

a. **Think** about the type of person you would like to meet.

b. **Plan** how you are going to meet your future partner e.g. be more sociable, etc.

c. **Strategise** by choosing activities that will increase your chances in meeting your future partner.

d. **Execute** by regularly implementing your chosen strategy.

e. **Re-evaluate** the outcomes of your strategies. For example, are you going to the right places to meet your future partner?

## ✱ Speed up the Process

Can you actually realise your life answers in a shorter timeframe? Well of course, there are some things you can choose to do.

## ☑ Apply Positive Affirmation

Positive affirmation involves the channeling of positive energies or thinking into the universe with the hope that this will increase the chances of realising your life answers.

For example, let's say you have set yourself a goal to buy a new home by the end of the year. Write this goal down on a piece of a paper:

*'I will buy my house by the end of the year'*

Display this piece of paper somewhere prominent or visible where you will be able to see it on a daily basis. You can even record it on a media to play back on a regularly basis.

By frequently seeing and hearing it, you are putting the positive energies of buying a house into the universe. Soon you will start attract the energies of buying a new home to your life.

## ☑ Embrace the Power of Connectivity

If you want something to happen sooner, you can embrace the power of connectivity which involves being around the right place, right people and at the right time. To do this, you will need to carefully strategise your available options and choose the condition/s that will maximise the chances of realising your life answers.

## ☑ Surround Yourself with Energy Colours

If you want your life answers to be realised sooner, then surround yourself with bright energy colours such as orange or yellow. Bright colours can help to attract positive energies into your life.

However, there is a danger to surrounding yourself with too much energy colours for too long. It can drain you. So be careful not to over expose yourself with these energy colours.

## ☑ Program Your Crystals

Crystals have been known to contain a special type of energy within them. Some crystals can be programmed to improve general health. Others can be programmed to help address a certain issue in your life. For example, yellow crystals can stimulate activity or promote speed.

So how do you program a crystal? There are many techniques but there is one that I would recommend.

Firstly, to cleanse your crystal, soak it in salt water. Next, energise your crystal. You can do this by putting it under the moonlight overnight. Once the crystal is charged, you can begin the programming process by placing it on your hand and start channeling your energy to it - in this instance 'the realisation of my life answers'. You can also mentally imagine the energy channeling process to the crystal.

Once the crystal is programmed, do not allow anyone to touch it as he/she can contaminate the energy. Keep it close to you.

## ☑ Leverage on the Art of Feng Shui

Feng Shui has been practiced by the Chinese for many centuries. It involves studying the flow of energies (chi). It can be used to attract positive energy flows if you know how to use it effectively. For example, by putting Chinese gold coins in your wallet, you will attract more wealth and prosperity.

## ☑ Pursue a Healthy Mind and Body

A healthy mind and body is probably the most important aspect for an individual to live a fulfilling life. Therefore you should always eat well, exercise and maintain a positive lifestyle. If you have a healthy mind and body, you will have the foundation to pursue the realisation of your life answers.

# Start Living a Positive Life

# Start Living a Positive Life

Now that you have discovered the path to discovering and realising your life answers, why wait any longer?

It is time to live a fulfilling life!

# Maintain a Positive Life

# Maintain a Positive Life

Now that you are living the life that you have been dreaming of for a long time, you must ensure that you continue to maintain this positive attitude to life. Do not let any negative energy take over your life. You must remind yourself that you are in control. You can live this life of yours, the way you want it to be.

Remember:

- ☑ Always look at the positive side of life.
- ☑ You have nothing to lose - if you never try, you will never know.
- ☑ Expect the unexpected e.g. worst case scenario.
- ☑ Do not let yourself 'rot'. Life is too short to sit around and do nothing.
- ☑ Surround yourself with positive people who can give you the encouragement and support.
- ☑ Have confidence in yourself!

# About Find My Life Answers

Find My Life Answers Pty Ltd is a company dedicated to promoting a positive approach to finding life answers.

For more information about the company, please visit www.findmylifeanswers.com.

www.ingramcontent.com/pod-product-compliance
Lightning Source LLC
Chambersburg PA
CBHW050348290526

45785CB00006B/2691